Suicide

ALSO BY NGOZI OLIVIA OSUOHA

The Transformation Train
Letter to My Unborn
Sensation
Tropical Escape (with Amos O. Ojwang')
Fruits from the Poetry Planet
Poetic Grenade
Whispers of the Biafran Skeleton
Chains
Raindrops
Freeborn
Eclipse of Tides
The Subterfuge
Green Snake on a Green Grass
Chariots of Archangels
Wonderment
Interwoven
xenophobicracy
Destiny
The Phenomenal Human
Christmas Fever

Suicide

poems by
Ngozi Olivia Osuoha

Poetic Justice Books
Port St. Lucie, Florida

©2020 Ngozi Olivia Osuoha

book design and layout: SpiNDec, Port Saint Lucie, FL
cover image: *'pale Wizard*, 2018, Kris Haggblom

All rights reserved.

No part of this book may be used or reproduced in any manner whatsoever without written permission except in the case of brief quotations embodied in critical articles and reviews. Members of educational institutions and organizations wishing to photocopy any of the work for classroom use, or authors, artists and publishers who would like to obtain permission for any material in the work, should contact the publisher.

Published by Poetic Justice Books
Port Saint Lucie, Florida
www.poeticjusticebooks.com

ISBN: 978-1-950433-58-2

FIRST EDITION
10 9 8 7 6 5 4 3 2 1

*This poetry book is dedicated
to all the victims of suicide.*

contents

Heartbreak	3
Hunger	4
Disppointment	5
Loss	6
Hate	7
Segregation	8
Frustration	9
Trauma	10
Umemployment	11
Failure	12
Several Attempts	13
Loneliness	14
Boredom	16
Gossip	17
Divorce	18
Cheating	19
Betrayal	20
Scandals	21
Nudity	22
Blackmail	24
Snub	25
Deceit	26
Orphaned	27
Retrenchment	28
Dismissal	29
Mental Health	30
Depression	31
Anger	32
Bitterness	33
Jealousy	34
Envy	35
Greed	36
Discouragement	37
Disengagement	38
Death of Fiance	39
Infatuation	40

False Living	41
Ungodliness	42
Rumour	43
Low Self Esteem	44
Faithlessness	45
Hopelessness	46
Desperation	47
Poverty	48
Murder	49
Rape	50
Injustice	51
Prejudice	52
Imprisonment	53
Sack	54
Hard Labour	55
Restlessness	56
Unfaithfulness	57
Slavery	58
Racism	59
Religion	60
Fear	61
Attack	62
Spiritual Manipulation	63
Terror	64
Heredity	65
Mercy Killing	66
Terminal Disease	68
Society	69
Freedom	70
Recklessness	72
Peer Pressure	73
Poor Parenting	74
Duping	75
Unwanted Pregnancy	76
Loan	78

Melt Down	79
Delay	80
Marriage	81
Over Pampering	82
Over Discipline	83
Persecution	84
Sex for Grade	85
Cultures	86
Comparison	88
Open Up	90
Be Strong	91
Stress	92
Written Off	94
Challenges	95
Heroes	96
Voices	97
Books	98
Movies	99
Social Media	100
Bullying	101
Bet	103
Violation	104
Revenge	105
Prayer	106
Loving	107
Equity	108
Patience	109
Discover Your Purpose	110
Suicide	111
about the author	113

Suicide

HEARTBREAK

When it is soft and loud
Towering to the cloud
You dare not listen to the crowd
Because suddenly it can go sour.

Love can blindfold
Making one so cold,
Like a cruise control
You loosen the nuts.

But when the worst happens
Cheating, betrayal or disappointment
Lies, theft, duping or kidnapping
You weep uncontrollably
Regretting ever loving.

Then the thoughts vary
Voices speaking, and condemning
Decisions running through.

Suicide sings, choices echo
Contemplation tangles,
But suicide, never an option.

It must surely calm
Nothing boils forever
Dust always settle down.

HUNGER

Hunger is a beast
It kills hope
Hunger is a monster
It rapes faith.

Hunger is a witch
It stagnates growth
Hunger is a wizard
It strangles development.

Yes, hunger kills
It bewitches, it hurts
It retards, it stunts
Hunger is evil.

But hunger is temporary
It comes and goes
Hunger is not everlasting
It has an expiry date.

Hold on, dear
Stay put, time provides
Suicide is not the option.

You can conquer
Yes, you, this you can win
Only a little more patience
Success will be up with the moon.

DISAPPOINTMENT

Lean not on men
For they are mortals
Hold not unto women
For they fade away
All things change
Nothing is permanent.

Disappointment comes, it goes
Disappointment can be disastrous
Yes, it is shocking
It is heartbreaking
It overwhelms
But it never lasts.

Disappointment is a teacher
It teaches and corrects
It points out factors
Factors of factual facts
Separating fictions from realities,
Focus on the realities
Let the fictions go,
Suicide is not an option.

LOSS

Loss is loss
It is a gain, sometimes
Loss can take you unawares
It can come wrongly
It can come rightly,
But loss is a part of life.

Loss of friendship, love
Loss of partner, colleague
Loss of a parent
Loss of a relative
Loss is an unseen entity
Dwelling amongst men
Felt, known, yet unseen.

Loss of expertise
Loss of merchandise
Loss of wealth or health
Losses abound.

Hold on, be strong
We outgrown loss
When we move on.

HATE

Hate is not new
People hate, people are hated
Hate is not new
In the beginning, it was there.

Forget hate and hatred
Let them hate, live on
Align your soul with God
Capture your dream
Live your purpose
Hate is a distraction.

Love yourself, that is real
Feed your spirit, live on
Water your soul, hang on
Lead on, roll on, row on
Continue the hustle
It will pay someday,
Enjoy life, make a statement
Suicide is not for you.

SEGREGATION

They will segregate
They will prefer and refer
They will intimidate
They will frustrate,
But look away from them.

Segregation is unfair
Discrimination too, is
But you are just you
The only one to prove them wrong
Live it, do it, believe it
Segregation too can be intimidated.

Whatever their pattern
However, their method
Wherever, their strategy
Whenever, they hit
Look away, ignore them
Dance with your brain.

FRUSTRATION

Life is not straight
It is zigzag and spiral
Nothing comes easy, especially good things
Including the ones we deserve
So prepare for anything.

When it hits, heat up
When it strikes, warm up
When it attacks, stay fit
Frustration is a cantonment.

Be prepared, be bold, be ready
Be humble, stay at alert
Frustration comes in colours
Friends, jobs, hunger, calling
Dreams, relatives, travels, tours and more.

Frustration is also a key
It can direct, redirect
It can lead, point, guide
Always learn the good in all.

Suicide is not the pathway
Time heals, time saves, time rescues,
Say no to suicide
Tomorrow will be great.

TRAUMA

It is ravaging
With several thoughts running
Tearing the heart to pieces
Scaring the soul apart
Rending the body into bits.

Heartbreak in diverse forms
Trauma in many shades
Up, down, left, right, center
In relationship, in job,
In housing, in allowance
In past, in present, in future
Heartbreak and trauma, a stumbling rock.

But move on, look up
You are a giant
Giant at heart, in head
You are a hero, hero at large
Face up, lean on, cheer up.

Heartbreak recks apart
Trauma can be outrageous
It can be a duping deadline
But say no to suicide,
It only transfers the pain
The huger part of it.

UNEMPLOYMENT

Idleness is the devil's workshop
It can lead to anything,
Unemployment kills
Especially when you are qualified
When your mates are better
And you lag behind
Or seem to be backward.

Unemployment is a cage
It restricts growth
Unemployment is a cave
It confines movement
But then there is God
No matter what.

Death is an inevitable end
But never make haste to die
For there is a time for everything
Time breaks chains
And time limits, limits.

Ngozi Olivia Osuoha

FAILURE

Failure is a teacher
It helps to expand knowledge
Failure is not the end
Rather a bend to divert.

Failure is part of life
It guides success too
Failure is a train
Humans board it
Intentionally or not.

No matter how many times you fail
There is a lesson to be learnt
Unlock it, find it
It is a secret, sometimes a treasure
The light shines after the tunnel.

Failure does not murder
Despite the harm
Failure does not kill
Irrespective of the delay
Sometimes failure is a compass
It leads the voyage of our discovery.

SEVERAL ATTEMPTS

People attempt severally
They try always,
They fight now and then
Yet they move on.

Several attempts may fail
One attempt may succeed
Whichever, it is not the end.

Brace up, cheer up
Hang on, ride on, row on
The wave of life is not steady
Time and tide hide and seek
Storms pass away.

Lean on, learn on, try on
Live it, live up, live real
Suicide is a deceit
It takes away brighter future.

LONELINESS

We are created different
Born different
But all human.

Humans need companies
They make companies,
They are companies.

Loneliness is a threat
It bores, it hurts
But in loneliness
Visions mature
Creativity explodes
Revelations float
Dreams rise
Prayers thrive
Maturity survives.

Loneliness calls for discernment
Say no to suicide
For life is worth more than materials.

Drug and alcoholism
Escape routes from boredom and loneliness
They only worsen matters.

They destroy lives
They create addicts
And rapists.

Stay away from drugs
Alcohol and alcoholism
Those ruin, too.

Forget temporary pain
And immediate pain relief
They coil back
And launch deeper
Destroying more and more
So stay away from drugs
Do not befriend alcohol.

BOREDOM

Boredom is a trap
It can catch the wise
Boredom is a track
It can play the gentle
Boredom is a prank
It can come for the humble
Boredom is a well
It can swallow the kind,
But boredom is not God.

Bore your boredom
Bore it till it leaves
Engage yourself
Sing, play, write, stroll
Pray, workout, hang out
Boredom is manageable.

Suicide is not everything
Get rid of it
Just a little while, all will be well.

GOSSIP

Gossip hurts
It harms reputations
Gossip demoralizes
It dents characters.

When gossip flies
When gossipers write
When gossip explodes
When they merry
When they celebrate
It can be alarming.

Shun them, ignore them
Be strong and bold
You are a warrior
A giant on earth
Searching for giant-dom
Look beyond their words
Turn it to your own good.

Say no to suicide
It hurts the living
When you are gone,
Gone crazily
The living gets crazier.

Ngozi Olivia Osuoha

DIVORCE

Divorce is not a crime
But it can break
Divorce is not a sin
But it can crush,
When it happens
Hold yourself together
No matter the love
No matter the sacrifice
Forget the regrets
Just push on.

Life is worth more than ruby
The living is hopeful
Only the dead is hopeless.

Divorce is not a ceiling
What will be will be
Divorce always finds us
It does not make us the ugliest
Or the most cruel,
Be still, be strong, be lively
Suicide is not the ultimate.

It is never easy
It hurts, it is painful
But time heals well
And sometimes a better companion,
Say no to suicide.

CHEATING

Cheating pains
It hurts, it hurts
Especially to the faithful.

Cheating is demeaning
It reduces, it debases
Especially to the godly.

Cheating is regrettable
It flogs, it taunts
It accuses, it alleges
Especially to the meek.

Cheating punishes
It severs, it separates
It belittles, it defames
Especially to the decent.

Kill not yourself
A good name is better than death,
Nothing lives forever
Victim or suspect
Nobody is perfect
We are all humans,
Say no to suicide.

Ngozi Olivia Osuoha

BETRAYAL

Betrayal is crazy
It leads to sorrows
Betrayal is agonizing
It can cause more harm.

Betrayal is deadly
Because it comes from within
An enemy does not betray
Only friends, colleagues and relatives can.

Terrible betrayal can do evil
Mild betrayal can, too
Let us handle all with care.

Suicide is not the greatest
Time takes care of all
Patience provides soothing
Only a little while
The wave will die down
And you would rise
Rise, rise, amidst the storm.

SCANDALS

Scandals are forceful
They can pull the mountain
Scandals are strong
They can push love away
Scandals are great
They can torment
Scandals are ugly
They can damage.

Be cheerful in times of scandals
Control your emotions
Ride over the storm
Pray for grace
Do not take your life.

Scandals ruin thoughts
They bring ruining suggestions,
The mind filters and interprets
But always choose wisely,
Nothing, good or bad lasts forever
Not even the ugliest situation.

NUDITY

When we do funny things
And act silly,
When we go beyond normalcy
And exhibit stupidity
Knowingly or unknowingly
Forcefully or willingly,
Life can correct us.

Nudity is sacred
Unfortunately, it is stardom
It brings fame and favour
Instead of shame and lame,
It gives name and noise
Irrespective of the nuisance.

So when we act to fly
To reach a certain destination
By appearing nude or giving nude,
When those actions fly
Instead of us, flying
When the world sees them
And unveils who we are
Secretly, openly, especially secretly
We think crazy, crazy thoughts.

Be courageous, still then
It dies with time
Be bold, grow up
Mistakes are human
Growth is celestial,

Suicide

Necessary lessons we learn
Proper cautions we take
Especially through life.

Say no to suicide
Suicide cannot stop it,
Cheer up, grow up
Be strong, time will attend to you.

Ngozi Olivia Osuoha

BLACKMAIL

Blackmail is dark
It paints evil
It scares, it frightens.

The blackmailer is happy
He is bold and proud
He is ungodly and indecent
Capitalizing on mistakes.

Blackmail is poisoning
It cooks stories
It frames pictures
It produces hurts
And threatens coverage.

The blackmailer is mean
Ready to do his worst,
But take him by surprise
Open up to the right people
Contact the appropriate powers
Shame the devil.

Say no to suicide
It does not worth it,
The future is bright,
Yes, brighter than we can imagine.

SNUB

We are humans
We make choices
We have rules
We have principles,
And we try to go by them.

When snubbed, move on
When let down, go on
When treated unfairly, go.

Snubbing is rude
Snubbing is immaturity
But then, move on.

Loving is not by force
Friendship is not by force
Marriage is not by force
Accept change, brace up.

Anybody can snub anybody
Great, small, big, little
Religious, political, social, legal
Life goes on.

Ngozi Olivia Osuoha

DECEIT

Deceit is many
It comes from anywhere
Do not harm yourself.

Deceit injures
It wounds
It disappoints
And dislocates
But, harm not yourself.

Learn to move on
For moving on is the map
Growing is the true love
Letting go is the secret.

Deceits will come
From far and wide,
Even from unexpected quarters
Be ready, be prepared
Just count suicide out.

ORPHANED

Life can be hopeless
Especially when the future looks dim
When there is no father
When there is no mother
No one to help
No one to advise
None to run to
Chances of pain grow.

Orphans see hell
They pass through horrors
Their sorrows are enormous,
Only God trains them

So when life happens
When nature cheats you
When life appears hateful
And living, illogical
Please say no to suicide.

Suicide is regrettable
But to those who survive it,
Suicide leaves more pain
To those who mourn,
Say a big no to suicide.

RETRENCHMENT

Life is hard
It is not easy anywhere
Life is unfair
It is not fair anyhow,
But some are lucky
Some are blessed
Some carry on, wise.

Retrenchment is horrible
It can cause death,
Retrenchment is disastrous
It can frustrate,
Especially the one unnecessary
The one avoidable,
The one unmerited
The one unwarranted.

When retrenched, sacked
When forced to resign
When laid off, please stay alive
Suicide is not the solution.

Sometimes, God rescues us
Yes, from dangerous work
Known or unknown to us,
Then sooner or later, He settles us,
Say no to suicide, therefore
For life is bit by bit.

DISMISSAL

Dismissal is heartbreaking
No matter how it comes
Lost years put in
Passion, time, work
Services, friendship, name
All, gone in a twinkle.

It can brew suicide thoughts
It can call for contemplation
Dismissal can be haunting.

In times like such
Do not throw in the towel
Move beyond circumstances
Look above temptations
Always believe in God,
Suicide does no good
No, not one.

Ngozi Olivia Osuoha

MENTAL HEALTH

Health is great
It is good that we be healthy
We need good health to carry on,
Because health is wealth.

But when sickness strikes
When health is questioned
When safety is challenged,
When sanity is objected
Then tears flow down.

Mental health is real
We need it to be alert
We need it to stand
When otherwise, troubles set in.

When grossly traumatized
Please hold on, be strong
Open up, speak out
Stay put, stay put
Suicide is a deceit
It ends it not,
Rather it passes it on.

DEPRESSION

Depression is real
It can kill, it has killed many
It is not visible
Nor written on the face,
Manage your life properly
Seek help, you will get it.

Look out for friends
Watch out for relatives
Embrace one another, love people
Depression is mental.

Unseen, unheard, unknown
It goes around destroying
Igniting trauma and pain
Chaining lives and love.

Depression is a bondage
It incapacitates, it binds
It kills, it hurts, it demoralizes
But suicide never cures anything.

ANGER

Anger is nature
It is real and normal
Negative anger
Positive anger
Righteous anger
Unrighteous anger,
All, any, can be productive.

All takes anger to create
Anger too, it takes to destroy
Control your anger
Manage yourself
Discipline your emotions
Lead and rule your all
Do your best even at worst
For suicide is not holy.

Anger can cause suicide
When broken, bruised
When annoyed, disappointed
When belittled, ignored
Anger can be devastating.

Yes, it is normal to be angry
But burn not yourself,
Let it pass
For time deals with everything.

BITTERNESS

Bitterness steals joy
It engulfs happiness
Bitterness fluctuates calmness
It pollutes tenderness.

Stay alive, stay lively
Stay agile, stay alert
Bitterness is a demonic trap.

Bitterness is cunning
It creeps in gradually
And stays longer
Never give it a seat
Lest it takes your soul.

Forget suicide, it pays not
Look forward, move higher
Backward never, upward we go.

JEALOUSY

A can of worms
Deceiving ghost
It is a monster
Small but mighty,
Jealousy, a complex evil.

It is tender, smooth
It appears normal and normal
Digging for the heart
Reaching for the soul
Creating enmity
Silently encouraging
Until it explodes.

Jealousy is not good
Kill it, silence it forever
It is a burden of monster
Chase it far away.

ENVY

Envy is very slippery
It is a mountain
High, fearful, abnormal
It can kill the climber.

Unguided steps, death
Unguarded moves, death
Uncheckmented thoughts, death
Ward off envy, it is sickening.

Envy comes with bitterness
It gives jealousy
It creates sadness
It tears apart
Envy, is a deadly zone.

Suicide may fling in
Fling it out at once
Suicide may rear up
Sweep it off immediately.

GREED

Greed is a fighter
An unnecessary fighter
Even when it is at fault.

It yells, it screams, it shouts
It pretends, it scatters
It mocks, it betrays
It does anything anytime
It goes anywhere anyhow
It never minds
It cares not, it just not
Greed is solely ready.

Gored oxen, stepped toes
Slit throats, bleeding hearts
Greedy moves unconcerned.

Let it not enter
Wage it outside, overboard
Suicide can come along
Send them packing.

DISCOURAGEMENT

Many struggles to cope
Many attempts to survive
Many fights to grow
Many prayers to excel
Many sacrifices to live
Much hope to make it
But then no encouragement.

Attempts, struggles, fights
Prayers, sacrifices, hope
But discouragement in return.

Discouragements are frustrating
They draw the battle line
They pull the trigger
Only the strong dodge them.

But then suicide is not cool
Say no to suicide.

DISENGAGEMENT

Love is a beautiful thing
When you find your heartthrob
You fly without wings
It seems like you are in heaven
You praise the creator
And thank nature for blessing you.

When you find your true love
You announce it everywhere
You blow the trumpet
Sound the timbrel
And ring the alarm,
You wish for life and good health
You pray for prosperity.

But when the table turns
When there is disengagement
When a trouble cracks in
Then suicide peeps through the window.

Yet, you can win
Say no to suicide
It does not pay.

DEATH OF FIANCÉ

Death is a mighty blow
It takes men unawares
Death is a whirlwind
It scatters and shatters.

Death is horrible, it hurts
It devastes and traumatizes
When a loved one dies
Thoughts run up and down.

Shock is alarming
It horrifies, and terrifies
It creates doubts and denials
But then it is a bitter reality.

Death of a fiancée or fiancé
Death of a loved one
Death of a young lover
Can lead to suicidal thoughts.

But it is only for awhile
Nothing lasts forever
Blessed are they that mourn
For they shall be comforted.

Say no to suicide
Be strong, be strong
The winds will die down
Together with the waves,
And the storm shall give up.

INFATUATION

When infatuated
We float in fantasy
We appear sailing
But a little wave
Wave of reality
The bubble bursts
And we realize
Our foolishness
And suicide comes ringing.

Infatuation is a bubble
It is a beautiful balloon
Colourful and big
But burst-able, breakable.

Say no to suicide
A little time, heals
A little patience, saves
Life can offer better things ahead.

FALSE LIVING

Faking a lifestyle
Claiming what one is not
Appearing rich when and while poor
Forgery and misgivings
Those can lure suicide.

Lies, deceits and betrayals
Framing stories to get something
Especially something uncalled for,
Posing to be a king
When one is a pauper
Can force one to think of suicide
Even directly or indirectly.

Because when exposed
When disgraced
When punctured
When ruptured and deflated
Shame, ego, pride,
Regret, anger, disappointment
And other things can invite suicide.

Ngozi Olivia Osuoha

UNGODLINESS

Life is a mystery
We barely know a little
Destiny is more mysterious
We are just representatives
Forces govern the world
Sometimes, they manipulate us
It needs spirituality
Apart from other realms.

We need to focus on God
To ascertain our purpose
The reason we are here
Otherwise we derail.

Hence ungodliness can kill
If we deviate recklessly
If we fly godlessly
At a point anger may strike
And we land on suicide.

But we can win
No matter what
If we open up
And look unto God.

RUMOUR

Rumours are great
They can foil plans
And crumble souls
They fly far and wide
And have the tendency to destroy
They can ruin reputations.

Rumours just pop up
They disseminate speedily
Even when the victims are unaware
And sometimes totally innocent.

Rumours are very harmful
They kill morale and spirit
They quench zeal and hope
Rumours scatter, and shatter
They can cause suicide
Whether true or false.

Yet, say no to suicide
It is not worth it,
Never, just a little time
The enemy will be put to shame.

Ngozi Olivia Osuoha

LOW SELF ESTEEM

Low self esteem is a dent
It stains apparels
No matter how costly.

Low self esteem is deadly
It belittles, it cripples
It mocks, it humiliates.

Low self esteem is bad
It deceives, it betrays
It hurts, it fools.

Low self esteem is ugly
It blinds, it blindfolds
It takes away confidence
It buries boldness
And wards off courage.

Low self esteem is unfair
It can kill, it frustrates
It forces one to believe wrongly
And conclude stupidly
Having dirty deductions.

FAITHLESSNESS

Faith climbs mountains
Faith gives hope
Faith believes possibilities
Even when there are no chances.

Faith catapults the spirit
It gingers the unseen
It gathers the unknown
It builds the invisible.

Faith shares calmness
It gives serenity
It comforts and consoles
Faith just rescues.

But faithlessness says otherwise
It believes all is gone
It concludes no need to live
It can commit suicide
So say no to suicide
Have faith
Move those mountains
You can make it.

HOPELESSNESS

Life can be crazy
Especially when things are not working
Life can be suicidal
When friends betray.

When efforts yield no result
When hard works perish
When businesses fall apart
When realities dawn on us
Ugly realities that question
Life can be meaningless.

Hopelessness can point at suicide
It can force one to try it,
It can compel even the holiest.

Hopelessness can becloud
Yes, it can
And then everything will be dim
Yet, say no to suicide.

DESPERATION

Desperation can kill
Yes, it can
Especially when unnecessary.

Desperation is a deadly tool
When used wrongly
It can have adverse effect.

Desperation must be managed
And geared towards good
Otherwise it pushes off.

Over desperation is a bomb
It explodes automatically
It is devastating and agonizing.

Desperate situations may need it
Desperate people must be careful
Because desperation can be evil.

When desperate moves fail
When they prove abortive
When they frustrate even more
Please say no to suicide.

Ngozi Olivia Osuoha

POVERTY

Poverty is a terrible thing
It lures one to many things
Poverty is a disease
It needs serious cure,
Poverty seems like a curse
Even without cause,
Poverty is deadly
It frustrates, it handicaps.

Poverty is annoying
It can paralyze dreams
Poverty is dangerous
It can cripple future,
But poverty can be fought and won.

Helpless, hopeless, cheerless
Lonely, hungry, thirsty
One can think stupid
But poverty can be fought and won.

It can be conquered
Say no to suicide
Fight and win poverty,
Make history, you can.

But also remember
Poverty is a mindset
Money is not all about riches
Gifts, talents are wealth too.

MURDER

Blood is thicker than water
Blood speaks, yes it does
Unthinkable things happen
Mysteries and puzzles
The world is full of wonders.

Some commit murder
Some kill willingly
Some kill accidentally
Some secretly, some openly.

Murder is a crime
No one gets away with it
Especially when caught
But uncaught, it haunts
It torments and taunts
A confession can help
It will go a long way
Say no to suicide
It is not the solution.

Ngozi Olivia Osuoha

RAPE

Rape is a crime
It is a humiliation
It is a big violence
Violence and violation against humanity.

Rape is evil, it traumatizes
Only a few get over it,
A very strong few
Coupled with grace,
Special grace.

Many things are attached to it
Disease, pregnancy, shame
Defilement, abuse, broken vows
Stigmatization, taboo, desecration, hate
And other terrible issues.

Many commit suicide after rape
Because the guilt is too much
The anger is great
They feel useless and worthless
Hence they take their life.

Do not rape anyone
Help rape victims
Take away stigmatization
Reject victimizing victims
Stop the gossip, rumour, scandals and blackmails
Help victims heal.

Say no to suicide
Prevent suicide,
You can make a huge difference.

INJUSTICE

The world is terrible
Evil hatches, evil grows
From east to west
From north to south
Nowhere is truly safe.

Injustice spreads, it germinates
Injustice, official and unofficial
Injustice, legal and illegal
Cultural, non cultural, religious
Academic, traditional, health
All kinds of injustice
Especially against the poor.

Injustice traumatizes, it kills
It dwindles, it saddens
It is wickedness and hate
It can lead to self destruction.

But however, whatsoever
Time vindicates, dead or alive
No matter when, where and how.

Say no to suicide
It is not worth it,
Be patient, be strong
Be futuristic, be courageous
Tomorrow has your pay.

PREJUDICE

Ugly assumption
Bad conclusion
Wrong deduction
Unfair belief against one.

Concluding negatively
Judging before hand
Condemning ignorantly,
Forming adverse opinions against one
Because of colour, religion, race
Country, background, beliefs,
Setting barriers against people
Collectively or individually
Because of stories, perception, motives
This is harmful and deadly
It has done more harm than good
And still does.

Prejudice has killed many
It is still killing
Say no to prejudice
You would have prevented suicide.

IMPRISONMENT

Imprisonment is old
It did not start today
Some use it against others
Some use it to correct evil
But some use it to intimidate.

Some use it as power
Some as right, will
Some use it as honour
Some as crown and throne
But imprisonment should not be so.

Many are wrongly imprisoned
Many are untimely imprisoned
Many unduly, lengthy
Many, as transferred aggression
They use it the way they choose
Not minding the harm
The evil it causes on innocent people
Especially the poor and meek.

Wrong accusations and actions
Wrong allegations and reactions
Wrong judgements and imprisonments
They and their likes
Have done horrible evil to lives.

They can cause suicide
They can compel one to end it all
They can useless lives,
But then suicide is not the option.

SACK

People work to survive
They struggle day in, day out
They pray to be favoured
They wish to be promoted
They want the best
And they want to be the best,
No matter what.

People suffer, people enjoy
Sometimes, against our will or prediction
But then life goes on.

Every work has its wage.
So every worker deserves his pay
Good, bad, small, big,
Great or tiny.

Sacking can kill
Many people have died from sacking
Either shock or suicide
Whether established or not
No one likes being sacked
Irrespective of the ill or situation,
Especially those who have put in their best.

HARD LABOUR

Labour is normal
It is associated with man
Man must work to survive,
To keep life going.

Labour varies, however
There are abnormal ones
The ones brought by wickedness
The ones forced down on people.

Hard labour is an abuse
Even when one takes it by oneself
Hard labour can frustrate lives
Not just the individual involved.

Watch labour, watch work
Moderate it, let it not be excess
Mental, physical, social, cultural
Economic, financial, generally
For too much of everything is bad.

Hard labour can frustrate one into suicide
When one loses interest in work and working
When work becomes burden, burdensome
When it turns very cumbersome
Suicide may ring the bell to end it.

Say no to suicide
Save your life
Keep fit, look upward
Tomorrow will be great.

RESTLESSNESS

Restlessness is a torture
It can aggravate hate
Self hate and general hate
Bitterness and anger,
Hence the need for rest.

Rest resuscitates us
It helps us relax
It helps the body to chill
To break and make its cycle
And get ready to make it again.

Rest is vital
It is necessary and key
Without rest, one may achieve less
Despite the labour and resources,
And even die prematurely.

Rest, relax, play
Have leisure, Stoll
While away time sometimes
Go for sightseeing
So that suicide will die down.

UNFAITHFULNESS

Love is beautiful
It builds the body and soul
Love is pure
It cleanses the spirit,
Needless to contaminate it.

Love is green
It lives through time
Love is old
It grows forever,
It never dies.

Allow it, let it live
Leave it, let it blossom
Cheating is deadly
Infidelity is harmful,
Unfaithfulness pushes
It can push one to suicide.

Stay faithful, stay lovely
Stay truthful, stay pure
Say no to suicide.

SLAVERY

Slavery is a bond
It holds one captive
It binds, it chains
It uselesses, it punishes
It kills dreams and hopes
It wipes away future.

Slavery is a misfortune
It buries fortune,
Different slavery, different folks
Be not a slave
Keep not a slave
Be free, free others.

Say no to slavery
Say no to bondage
Be free, free others
Slavery is a blindfold.

People can commit suicide
If they discover they are slaves
Or if they be made slaves,
Say no to slavery
Stop bondage, stop suicide.

RACISM

Different people, different cultures
Different people, different colours
Black, white, Latino, Asian
From all walks of life.

The creator is amazing
Language, colour, culture
Yet, humans, mankind.

Put on earth for reasons
Be gentle, be civil, be humane
We are many, so many
Not just white, not just black.

Say no to racism
Racism is a hindrance,
Racial profiling is hate and prejudice
It is a stumbling block
It has killed many
It is still killing
Say no to racism.

Grow up, fly,
Reach out, learn, unlearn
Grow up, grow up
Racism is manmade.

RELIGION

Religion, the pathfinder
The pathway to God
Religion, the track, the tracker
The lane to the creator.

Tracks unknown, abounding
Paths, strange, so strange
Ways dynamic, confusing
Roads complicated, complex
Maps, a web
Full of doubts, beliefs
Questions, wonders
Religion, crazy, crazy.

Religion, suicidal
Religion, fomenting trouble
Wrong teachings, blasphemy
Brainwashing, deceit
Selfish, selfishness, hidden interest
Ulterior motives, greed, lust
Say no to covetousness.

Say no to suicide
Say no to suicide mission,
Live your life
Achieve your goals
Make your dreams flourish
Enjoy your stay on earth,
Let nobody dictate your end.

FEAR

Fear is a bondage
It torments its victims
Fear is a furnace
It burns its contents.

Fear, fear, fear of the unknown
Fear over nothing
Fear over something
Fear of the past
Fear of the present and future.

Fear of ghost, fear
Mobid fear for anything
Fear and doubts
Doubts of medical results
Fear of health issues
But suicide is not all
Tomorrow is looking blessed.

ATTACK

Some have seizures
Epileptic seizures
Some have financial seizures.

Seizures can mean anything
Anything breaking and quenching
In life, in love, in passion
In dream, in marriage, in career
Some tag it different things.

Attacks, seizures, health issues
Ignorance too can be one
Lack, pain, loss can be
Failure is one, sure
But we need to manage it.

Say no to suicide
Needless dying when life is changing
Time, a little time
It all changes
Changes for good
And the beauty of it all would be seen.

SPIRITUAL MANIPULATION

The world is mysterious
Living in it is a mystery
It offers misery
Even from nursery.

Things happen, and unhappen
We learn from them
For those ready to learn.

Forces abound, uncountable
They have impact on creatures
And they alter creation.

Positive, negative, neutral
Forward, backward, up, down
Circle, circular, round, center
In different forms and shapes
Sometimes suicide is a spiritual manipulation
But then, it can be waged.

Know your God
He will guide you,
Hold on to Him
He will shield
He too, manipulates
He is the master manipulator.

TERROR

Terror is growing
It is advancing
Time is helping it
Technology broadens it
Science supports it
Day by day, terror
Gradually, we are losing it.

Terror, terrorism and terrorists
Terrorizing the world
Killing millions, destroying
Brainwashed humans
Mean elements
Greedy folks, ignorant lots
Working for their masters.

Terror, suicide bombers
Terrorism, with promises
And hopes of enjoyment,
Say no to suicide and killings
For heaven is not that way.

HEREDITY

Heredity is strong
It tells many tales
Founded on facts and fictions.

Some lineages commit suicide
Some families, some links
Suicide can be traced.

Suicide is not a good omen
Nobody is proud of it,
Even at the point of death.

Heredity, hereditary or inherited
Inheritance or acquisition
Death is a loss, not gain
No matter who, how, when, where.

Say no to suicide
Even traits and families
Lineages and generations
Anybody can break the chain.

Ngozi Olivia Osuoha

MERCY KILLING

Our world is lost
We are no longer safe
None can truly understand
Why it is actually so.

Killings of different shade
Innocently, ignorantly, proudly
Boldly, richly, poorly, logically
Legally, normally, unconcernedly
Businesslike, syndicates
And other unthinkable and unbelievable types.

Abortion has a degree
Credentials and certificates
Stillbirth, stillborn, premature
Born well, born bad, born full
Born in pieces, born in blood,
Any pattern, anywhere, anyhow.

Clinics, hospitals, professionals
Accepting, making money,
Researching on numerous ways
Ways of legalizing and aborting
Aborting babies and unborn futures.

Say no to this
Killing is evil
Abortion is ungodly,
Say no to suicide.

Suicide

Imagine the millions of babies aborted
They could have been great researchers
Mighty philosophers
Astronauts, heroes and legends
Presidents, world leaders
And discoverers of excellent things.

Say no to suicide
Kill not, killing is evil.

Ngozi Olivia Osuoha

TERMINAL DISEASE

Some people are sick
Sick, so sick that survival is doubtful
They are in so much pain
And their caregivers in intense pain
Monies and resources have been spent
Many appear to be total waste
And it is not giving hope,
So they decide to end it all
That everyone may have peace.

They end it and rest
To them, it is better
But the vacuum remains
The pain, the loss, the regret
The waste, the time, the pain
All, always come back pointing somewhere.

A little time can do wonders
Miracles are real
Healings can be spontaneous
Anything can happen anytime to anybody
Have faith, say no to suicide
It is difficult, yes
It is not easy, true
But just believe in God
He is a miracle worker.

SOCIETY

The society is boiled
It is hot and lifeless,
It is still boiling, in fact
Nothing good seems good
Nothing bad seems bad.

The society has gone
It is deteriorated and debased
The society has decayed and decomposed
Stinking and smelling
Oozing out unholy odour
Odours of blood
Blood of young and old,
Men, women and children
And the world moves on.

The society has refocused itself
To your tents O you all
Live your life, anyhow
Do your wish anytime,
Hence suicide is alarming.

Gather yourself well
Focus, focus, I say focus
Concentrate, forget the noise
Let us rebuild the society
Because time shall come
When it will no longer be safe
For anyone, not even the unborn.

Ngozi Olivia Osuoha

FREEDOM

Freedom, the freedom to be free
Everyone clamours for freedom.

Everyone, I mean everyone
Even the foetus in the womb
Everyone is fighting, struggling
To be left alone, to be recognized.

Tom, Dick and Harry
East, west, north and south
Freedom is knocking
We are knocking
Being knocked, knocked up and down
Off and on, on and off
Yet, freedom battles and baffles.

Freedom has brought us thus far
Freedom has dealt with us this evil
This freedom of greed and hate
Yet we are bent on freedom.

Freedom to bear arms
Arms to kill,
Freedom to be adults
Adults that are childish.

Freedom, excessive freedom
It has ruined, it is ruining
It will ruin yet.

Suicide

Unnecessary freedom can destroy
It can push down one
And force one to do the unthinkable,
Trim your freedom
Control freedom
It is growing nuts
And ruining lives,
Say no to silly freedom.

Ngozi Olivia Osuoha

RECKLESSNESS

When one is reckless
And lives anyhow,
Spending resources carelessly
And misusing means
Time would catch up with him.

Recklessness is a trap
It scares me to the bones
Especially when need be not
Because it is a ditch.

Recklessness is a shadow
Always following the one
It hardly leaves
But when it does
It must have been late.

Do not be reckless
So that suicide can be prevented,
Live within your means
Save means and materials
Be prudent and sensible.

PEER PRESSURE

Pressure is real and natural
It continues throughout life
Including peer pressure.

Peer pressure is the worst
It deals with young people mostly
It hammers armatures
Especially those without tap roots

Peer pressure is hot
It hurts the weak
And even the strong sometimes.

Know your lane
Define your picture
Foresee your future,
Do not yield to peer pressure.

Peer pressure is mostly negative
It pushes one to do stupid things
It can lead to waywardness
Except controlled timely.

It can cause suicide
Stay on course
Be on guard,
Off course and off guard are dangerous.

Ngozi Olivia Osuoha

POOR PARENTING

Poor parenting has killed many
Those whose background were poor
Shallow parenting
Poor rearing
Feeble raising
Weak foundation
And carelessness,
All those and more, destroy.

Nonchalant attitude
Reluctance and lack of concerns
Negligence and incompetence
Misconduct, mistreatment
Poor parenting is disastrous.

Laying evil foundation
Sowing discord among siblings
Planting discrimination
Preaching segregation,
Loving some over others
Showing hate and rage to other children
Those can force suicide on people.

Ignorant parents raise ignorant children
Porous parents raise porous children
Giving flimsy excuses and accepting such
Not disciplining children rightly
Looking away from dangerous news
Careless upbringing
Reckless home management
All affect children.

DUPING

Duping too, kills
Many have died of it
There are people who were duped
By friends, foes, relatives
Colleagues, strangers, known, unknown
They could not bear it
So they killed themselves.

Having laboured in vain
Having trusted stupidly
Being deceived intentionally
Having duped by friends
People die and end it.

The pain, the Shame, the regret
The warning, the sign, the burden
The wonderment and bewilderment
Many just end it
But suicide is not the ultimate.

Hold yourself together
When troubles of unequal strength rise
When trials and temptations knock
In any form, from any form
Please always remain calm
Know that suicide does not pay.

Ngozi Olivia Osuoha

UNWANTED PREGNANCY

When teenagers see changes
Changes in their bodies
They boil with passion and quest.

When nature visits them
Especially ignorantly, untimely
Unpreparedly, they jump up and down.

That way, it goes wrong sometimes
They land in trouble
And for the girls mostly
They take in unprepared.

They recall home, belief, religion
Rules and regulations, values and cultures
And when the boys disappear
Or deny responsibilities,
They think, they think, and think.

Some families disown such girls
Some families reject such pregnancies
Things happen, events unfold
Depression, rejection, dejection
Bitterness, loneliness, abandonment
Living becomes traumatic, disgusting
And thoughts ring round.

Suicide

Even some unfaithful spouses
When they commit some taboos
They feel like terminating their life
Because of shame, betrayal, regret and pain.

But we can help
We can save victims
At least by loving them
By consoling and comforting them.

Say no to suicide
Own up, life goes on
Time waves some things away.

LOAN

Some people take loan
Especially from the bank
Hoping to pay back
When the reason is met
And profitable too,
But with time, things scatter
Shattering their plans
And paying back becomes more problem,
Then they contemplate suicide.

It has happened to many
Many died that way,
Disturbances from the bank
The shame of not meeting up
The horror of being tormented
The humiliation of losing all,
Properties, buildings, cars
Name, goodwill, being ejected
Forcing them out of it
Some attempt suicide.

Yet, as understandable as their pain
Nothing actually justifies suicide,
It does more harm
It leaves the living forever traumatized
And the dead perpetually in bond.

Say no to suicide
Save us all the trauma,
Miracles happen
Life is amazing.

MELT DOWN

There are many types of melt down
Economic melt down is one
A horrible one at that.

Rich people hate poverty
They never feel like going down.

Some wealthy folks dare suicide
When they sense a melt down.

Even when it would not affect them
When it is just a mere prediction
When markets fluctuate
When factors change negatively
When businesses become partly stagnant
They attempt crazy thoughts.

Yes, some wealthy and healthy people
Some who could not imagine going down
They commit or attempt suicide
Because of economic melt down.

Forgetting that only change is constant
Good, bad, ugly, beautiful, all change
No condition is permanent.

Melt downs can sweep lives away
No matter the hugeness of the lives
No matter the strength and backups,
But we can say no to suicide
Knowing that times are not steady.

Ngozi Olivia Osuoha

DELAY

Delay is a force
It can be more forceful
And pressuring.

Delay requires patience
And endurance, and hope too
It grows our prayer life
As it refines virtues in us.

But not all know or understand
Not all are willing to wait
Or go through the training with it,
Some lack courage, morale and strength
Some want it now or never
Hence they do funny things.

Delay can harm
Marriage, education, career
Promotion, job, childbearing
And lots more, these frustrate
While waiting on or for them.

And in this time, things happen
Many die for various reasons
Including suicide,
But then it is not the best.

Say no to suicide
Delay sometimes brings the best
Delay comes with all necessary
Delay, may mean the hand of God
Destiny can only be delayed.

MARRIAGE

Marriage is a union
A union between lovers
This time around, bewildering lovers.

Many can commit suicide for marriage
Especially if not allowed to marry their lover
Irrespective of the reasons.

Marriage, even married people
Some have committed suicide
Either due to hardship or cruelty
Domestic violence, depression
Or more reasons unimaginable.

Sometimes, when marriage is seen as a rescue
It can turn to bondage
And then crazy things happen,
Please talk to someone
A confidant, open up
Do not take your life,
Nor another person's
Say no to suicide.

Ngozi Olivia Osuoha

OVER PAMPERING

Over pampering is deadly
It is not always good
Excessive pampering harms
It leaves one pompous
And feeling more important.

When the pampering reduces
Even by a bit or more
They think the world has crumbled
They feel abandoned and poor
They believe they are no more valuable
Intense feeling of rejection and dejection sets in
They conclude they have been hated
And the best is to end it.

Over pampering creates false ego
It leaves one floating like a balloon
Easily deflated, burst-able.

Do not over pamper, be moderate
Stop the impending doom
Love equally, generously
Live within your means.

OVER DISCIPLINE

Over discipline is bad
It is an abuse
It kills the spirit
And plants bitterness
It stamps grudges
And places resentment
It breeds a huge anger.

When people are over disciplined
They feel inferior
They lack confidence
And hardly stand up for themselves.

It can also make one nervous
They can be aggressive
And always offended
Unnecessarily irritated.

They see bad in all
And find fault everywhere
Then things become more difficult
They hardly love or open up
They cork their life and secret
Never spreading out.

That can lead to suicide
Do not correct excessively
Never punish with hate
Make room for love
Even amidst errors,
So that you can prevent suicide.

PERSECUTION

Persecution is hot
It pains flesh and bone
It hurts spirit and soul
And hinders growth sometimes.

Persecution is diverse
Within and without
Family, relatives, social,
Educational, political, spiritual
Mental, financial and others.

It burdens, it worries
It brings down, it does,
It takes special grace to overcome.

Be strong when going through it
Say no to suicide
It does not pay
A while, just awhile
It will all be over
And you will be happy again.

SEX FOR GRADE

When people are true and dedicated
When they are committed
Brilliant, intelligent, bright
When they are humble, loyal, diligent
When they should pass
Pass well without issues
They expect to sail through,
Even those that look up to them.

Sex for grade has killed many
Young, old, men and women
It has tarnished images
And crumbled reputations,
People have died secretly
And openly because of this.

Demanding sex from people
Because they must pass under or through you
Many a time, boomerangs
It hardly ends well.

When exposed the victims act funny
When caught or accused
Suspects look for a way out
Which could amount to suicide.

Say no to sex for grade
Stop the abuse and harassment
Say no to suicide.

Ngozi Olivia Osuoha

CULTURES

Some cultures are evil
They are barbaric
Some cultures are demonic
They came from hell
To inflict pain and sorrow.

Some marriage, burial
Mourning, childbirth
And other cultural rites and ceremonies
They are weird
They can force people to take their life.

People can think of suicide
If they feel frustrated or intimidated
Because these cultures contradict them
The entirety of mankind
And civility.

When no one listens, no one cares
No one advocattes, they can end it
Just to escape these horrors
And show them that they cannot
They will not, they need not
Because they should not.

Suicide

Archaic cultures that rip self worth
Ancient traditions that dehumanize
People can throw in the towel
And say bitter goodbyes.

Say no to suicide
Help people to stay alive
Waive mean cultures
Embrace civilization
Grow, let evil die down.

COMPARISON

Stop the comparison
It does not help
In fact, it does more harm than good.

Parents compare children
Children compare parents.
Relatives compare themselves
Colleagues, leaders, friends
All compare each other and one another
Unfortunately, on the bad note.

These comparisons are not healthy
They force unhealthy competition
And bring up enmity.

Unwanted struggles
Unpredictable jealousy
These comparisons breed them.

It boils hate
Cools unity
Mocks oneness
Severs bonds
Stop the comparison.

Suicide

They compel people and contrast them
Especially weak ones
It makes them poorer
They faint more, and go down deeper
They appear shallow and feeble
And that could make them attempt suicide.

Say no to unreasonable comparison
Say no to suicide,
Save the world.

OPEN UP

Open up my dear friend
Talk to someone, anyone
Let it out, it cures
Yes, it does wonders.

Talk to people about your problem
A solution can come
It may not even take long,
But know this
Others may bear it
They may laugh at you
They may mock you
But never mind.

Be strong, be ready
No matter how secretive it must be
No matter how confidential
Be bold, be strong, you will be fine.

Talk, open up, to your confidant
Religious, political, spiritual
Tutor, mentor, whoever
There can be a way forward
Say no to suicide,
It makes matters worse.

BE STRONG

Be strong, my friend
You can survive
Nothing lasts forever
Every situation fades with time
Good, bad, ugly, beautiful.

Be strong, be strong, dear
You can make it tonight
The night brings the morning
It is always darkest before dawn.

One more time, one more night
Just one more
Hold on, hang in, there
Never give up
It is your time to shine.

Be strong, cross over
It does not last
Be bold, be hopeful, be inspired
The world is waiting for your glory
Your breakthrough is here
Say no to suicide.

Head up, head up, move on
Your manifestation shall be glorious
You are beautiful
Gorgeous soul of divine peace
Say no to suicide!

STRESS

Stress is a problem
But we live with it
Because it is part of life.

Learn to ease off always
Rest, relax, play around
Forget your sorrow
Do no drugs
Because it does not help
Rather it blows it up.

Stress is not strong
We make it strong
We are stronger than all
No matter what we face on earth
Nothing is ever new.

We force it to last
By beating the gong
Which is very wrong.

Relax, see movies,
Play, go to relaxation centers
Stress kills because we compile it
Take a long walk
With or without a loved one
Enjoy the amusement parks.

Suicide

You would see stress disappearing
Say no to suicide
Stay fit, stay strong
Stay healthy, life is good.

Always find the light
No matter the length of the dark tunnel.

Ngozi Olivia Osuoha

WRITTEN OFF

People write people off
Sometimes due to character
Or poverty or anything,
Not knowing that life is a mystery.

People think it is by power or might
Because they are myopic
And very shortsighted.

They know not that time changes
That the rich also cry
That the future is unpredictable.

So when they write you off
Fear not, worry not, just focus
Your time is in destiny.

Never act stupid
Look away from pressure
Say no to suicide
The land is green.

Life is from above
We live it to please heaven
Not men,
Forgive them, move on
No matter how hard it seems
Suicide is the worst.

CHALLENGES

Challenges abound in life
It is sometimes overwhelming
It strikes hard and harder
It is worst when one is powerless.

Challenges grow up too
They advance in size and shape
With time they overpower
Especially if unchallenged.

Challenges can pose threats
Threats to life, love, study, health
But never mind, move on
Be strong.

Never kill yourself due to challenges
Take not your life, nor another's
Focus, ride on, climb higher, life is real
Turn by turn, we get compensated.

Ngozi Olivia Osuoha

HEROES

There are heroes today
They speak and we listen
There are also many heroes unknown
There are legends everywhere
We honour and respect them
There are giants also
We value and compliment them
But none of them were born that way
They passed through life
In fact, fire and brimstone.

They fought, they laboured
They hungered, they thirsted
They were traumatized too
Some of them gave up
In short the world gave up on some too
But today the same world worship them.

Some of them attempted suicide
Some thought of it,
Some escaped it
Some survived it,
But today, life smiled on them.

Please hold on, stay put
Say no to suicide
Your time will come.

VOICES

Many people hear voices
Different types of voice
Sometimes calling their names
Sometimes asking them questions
Compelling them to act.

Some people hear things
As if people are talking to them
Some voices always tell them about suicide.

Some obey, some rebuke
Some fear, some speak out
Some keep mute, some run
As if running would end it.

When you hear such, please consult people
Open up to psychologists, doctors
Your spiritual leaders, and mentors
Let people help you out
Never yield to strange voices
Demanding strange things
Let God save you.

Say no to suicide
However it may come
Receive power to overcome.

BOOKS

Reading is good
Books are wonderful
Learning is incredible
We need them all.

It is a therapy
It does wonders
We need books, reading.

It is necessary
It expands our vision
And helps us grow.

Reading is pleasurable
It heals, it saves
But there are times it destroys
So we must desist from those times
And those kinds of reading.

Reading harmful things kills
Exploring demonic notes endangers
Inculcating satanic books
And learning evil hurts,
They destroy beyond imagination
We should stay away from them.

Read healthy books
Concentrate on the good
Do not read above your spirit
For strong spirits can harm
Except God be with you.

MOVIES

Movies are good
But it depends
There are ungodly ones
The ones that corrupt.

Movies teach, they entertain
But some do horror things
Horrors that harm future
Future of even the unborn.

Stay away from evil movies
Keep them at arm's length
People focus on business
Only interested in money and profit
They build fame with anything
They care not,
They just connect the world
And rule it,
Destroying homes, values, morals.

Never mind them
Look away from their destructive moves
Say no to suicide
For movies too teach tricks
Playing pranks on youngsters especially
Only to destroy them finally.

Ngozi Olivia Osuoha

SOCIAL MEDIA

Social media, agent of change
A necessary tool for the world
An important channel of communication.

Unfortunately, it destroys
The disadvantages chasing the advantages speedily.

Social media is a blessing
But it seems it is becoming otherwise
People get threatened daily
That they seek to end it.

Please live your life offline too
Offline especially
Forget the craziness of the media
Fake things all over
Lies, deceits, set ups, hate, envy
Jealousy, greed, show, lust, silliness
Stupidity and insanity everywhere
Never let them pull you down.

Too many fake things
Breasts, hips, lips, marriage
Properties, friendship, all fake
Forcing ignorant ones to mourn
To ask questions beyond
To think their beautiful life is cursed,
Say no to social media fakery
Stay alive
Say no to suicide.

BULLYING

Bullying has killed many people
People as young as pupils
Pupils who knew not about life
Who never understood love
Who never learnt confidence
Strengths, ups, downs, weaknesses and life.

Bullying has killed many
Outlaws bullying young people
Old, young, male, female
People of colour, white, black, others.

Bullying in streets, schools
Parks, teams, religious places
Sometimes, victims keep mute
Until they take drastic actions
Actions that are horrible,
Parents and guardians see not
Sometimes their blindness facilitates it
When children expect loved ones to ask why
To check on them
To show them love and care
They get angry when disappointed.

Stop bullying, report every bully
No matter the threat
Say no to suicide
Life goes on
Life grows with time
And so do we grow too.

Yesterday is gone
Today too, will be gone
Expect a bright tomorrow.

Little children, fear not
You know nothing about life
Always talk to your parents
Siblings and favourite person
Open up, do not take your life
Sometimes, people are jealous of you
Your hair, colour, brain, beauty
Voice, brilliance, choice, coolness
They wish to have it but cannot
So they tease you to annoy you.

Never mind them, ignore them
Report them to your parents
Call the police, your future is involved
Never harm yourself
Stay away from them, if you can
You are better than them.

BET

Sometimes people bet
They bet with so many things
Even things that are vital.

Some bet with money, life
Wife, son, business, clothes, belongings
Cars, wears, labels, gold, diamond
And other valuables.

They have to give it up
When they lose
So at this point
They choose to die
They regret their actions
They wonder why they had not won
And feel betrayed, disappointed
Despite the chances,
They imagine how richer, and famous
They would have been.

Some commit suicide
Instead of fulfilling the bet
Or they fulfill it and die still
Because of the magnitude of the bet.

Please say no to suicide
It is horrible, it is a taboo
Man and God condemn it,
Stay away from betting
The one that is deadly
The one you cannot stand.

VIOLATION

Some people are molested
Some are abused, exploited
Humiliated, violated
Especially women.

In offices, schools, houses
Some by their relatives
Custodians, guardians, parents
Some even by their confidants.
Some by their role models
Mentors, heads, leaders
And people who should protect them.

Numerous abuses unreported
Some under oath and curse
Never to report or open up,
So many things swept under carpets
Carpets of unholy unions.

Some of these people kill themselves
Sometimes they cause disaster
And then end it all.

Please open up, speak out
Talk to someone, seek help
Call for rescue
Send a distress call
Help will surely come.

Say no to suicide
It does not solve the problem,
Rather it creates more.

REVENGE

Some people commit suicide
Either as revenge or for revenge
They kick it off
Because someone offended them
Or as a revenge.

Some do it to make a statement
Some, for some people
Some, against some people.

Suicide takes many shapes
Drinking poisonous substance
Shooting oneself
Blowing up oneself
Jumping into a lagoon
Falling intentionally from heights
Running into a moving vehicle
Hanging oneself
Different ways, methods and patterns
But then, it is never good
Never a good way to die
Because death is a loss
Especially death by oneself.

Life is very precious
Irrespective of what we go through
Just a tick of time
And everything turns.

Say no to suicide
Wait for your time
Life is turn by turn.

PRAYER

Yes, prayer can help
It motivates hope
And builds morale.

Prayers lift the soul
It guides the spirit
And encourages.

God uses prayers to sustain us
He hears, He listens
He strengthens, He answers.

Pray always, also hope
Ask for strength and peace
Pray for guidance and love,
God understands better.

Say no to suicide
Suicide hurts more
The living mourns deeper.

LOVING

Loving can help
Show love, show care
No matter who, and when
No matter how little
It goes a long way.

Loving goes far
It recalls, it supports
It gives a sense of belonging.

Live, love, love, live
Care, care, just care
Give, support, pray, interact
Mix up, flow, rapport
People need people around
Show concern, uplift people
Help talents, help the needy.

Love people as our Saviour taught us
Give, cherish, be patient with people
Live upright, support one another
Say no to suicide
Yes, you would be saying then.

Ngozi Olivia Osuoha

EQUITY

Equity is a mentor
It mentors people
Yes, it does
When equity is there
Nobody murmurs nor grumbles.

Let equity rule, let justice lead
Equity and equal rights
They create peace and harmony
They give our voice melody.

If equity is missing
There would be problem
When there is problem
People think of death,
Because you have created anger
Doubt, hate, rage in them
Their head directly or indirectly mocks them
Calling them never do well
Making jest of them.

Give equity, give equal rights
Give justice, give peace
Then life would be free.

PATIENCE

Time is allotted to all
Time to shine, time to die
Destiny is responsible.

Wait, work, and pray
Your time will come
Never live above your means.

Patience pays well
It is a virtue, a rare one
Wear it, live it, hope it.

Turn by turn, stage by stage
Phase by phase, one by one
It gets to everyone.

Say no to suicide
Hang on, be strong
Your time will worth it.

Ngozi Olivia Osuoha

DISCOVER YOUR PURPOSE

Discover your purpose
Yes, your purpose on earth
Follow your dreams
Make sure it is your vision
Dream big, dream well.

Follow your heart
Your head, your mind
Be with your brain all the time,
Do not run in any man's lane
Run your race
Live your dream
Take your path
Create history
Make bold your footprints
Watch your footsteps,
You will be satisfied.

It is not about money
Fame is vain and vanity
Discover who brought you here
And why you are here,
Do not follow others
No matter how they succeed
Be in your mission
Only then you will arrive,
Please say no to suicide
Maintain your mark
Your mark of positivity.

SUICIDE

Hey! Suicide, go away
Yes, you
You agent of darkness
Be far from the world
You did not create it.

Suicide, die and die again
Die, let humans live above you
Let them live and live again.

Dry, let people flourish
Let humans be
Let mankind exist boldly
You are not their creator
Be far away in the desert.

We shall live and not die
Our vine will blossom
Our barn shall flourish
Our coasts shall enlarge
Yes, you suicide have lost
Your grip is gone
And breath, dead
You lost, lost forever
Now and ages to come.

Shame on you, devourer
Shame, you monster
Harmful beast
Seeking to steal
You are cursed forever,
Amen and amen.

Ngozi Olivia Osuoha is a Nigerian poet, writer and thinker. A graduate of Estate Management with experience in Banking and Broadcasting.

She has twenty-one poetry books published in Kenya, Canada, the Philippines, USA, and others. She has also co-authored one (with Kenyan literary critic Amos O. Ojwang').

She has been featured in over sixty-five international anthologies and also has published over two hundred and fifty poems and articles in over twenty countries.

Many of her poems have been translated and published into other languages, including Spanish, Russian, Romanian, Polish, Khloe, Farsi, and Arabic, among others.

She has won many awards; she is a one time *Best of the Net* nominee, has been nominated for a *Pushcart Prize*, and she has numerous words on marble.